A House Between Homes

Kids in the Foster Care System

KIDS HAVE *TROUBLES* TOO

A House Between Homes:
Kids in the Foster Care System

What's Going to Happen Next?
Kids in the Juvenile Court System

I Live in Two Homes:
Adjusting to Divorce and Remarriage

When My Brother Went to Prison

When Daddy Hit Mommy

My Feelings Have Names

I Don't Keep Secrets

I Like Me

When Life Makes Me Mad

A Place Called Dead

When My Sister Got Sick

When My Dad Lost His Job

Sometimes My Mom Drinks Too Much

A House Between Homes

Kids in the Foster Care System

by Sheila Stewart and Camden Flath

Mason Crest Publishers

MASON CREST PUBLISHERS INC.
370 Reed Road
Broomall, Pennsylvania 19008
(866)MCP-BOOK (toll free)
www.masoncrest.com

First Printing
9 8 7 6 5 4 3 2 1

Library of Congress Cataloging-in-Publication Data

Stewart, Sheila, 1975–
  A house between homes : kids in the foster care system / by Sheila Stewart and Camden Flath.
      p. cm.
  Includes bibliographical references and index.
  ISBN (set) 978-1-4222-1691-0   ISBN 978-1-4222-1692-7
  ISBN (ppbk set) 978-1-4222-1904-1   ISBN (ppbk) 978-1-4222-1905-8
  1. Foster home care—United States—Juvenile literature. I. Flath, Camden, 1987– II. Title.
  HV881.S74 2010
  362.73'30973—dc22
                                      2010012756

Design by MK Bassett-Harvey.
Produced by Harding House Publishing Service, Inc.
www.hardinghousepages.com
Illustrations by John Ashton Golden Mortal Mirror Studio.
Cover design by Torque Advertising + Design.
Printed in USA by Bang Printing.

Introduction

Each child is unique—and each child encounters a unique set of circumstances in life. Some of these circumstances are more challenging than others, and how a child copes with those challenges will depend in large part on the other resources in her life.

The issues children encounter cover a wide range. Some of these are common to almost all children, including threats to self-esteem, anger management, and learning to identify emotions. Others are more unique to individual families, but problems such as parental unemployment, a death in the family, or divorce and remarriage are common but traumatic events in many children's lives. Still others—like domestic abuse, alcoholism, and the incarceration of a family member—are unfortunately not uncommon in today's world.

Whatever problems a child encounters in life, understanding that he is not alone is a key component to helping him cope. These books, both their fiction and nonfiction elements, allow children to see that other children are in the same situations. The books make excellent tools for triggering conversation in a nonthreatening way. They will also promote understanding and compassion in children who may not be experiencing these issues themselves.

These books offer children important factual information—but perhaps more important, they offer hope.

—*Cindy Croft, M.A., Ed., Director of the Center for Inclusive Child Care*

Micky slid down in the back seat of Stephanie's car. All her misery was jumping around in her body, making her heart pound, her stomach clench, and her brain feel like it was running in a million directions at once. The worst thing that could have happened had happened: they were putting Blake and Micky in different foster homes.

For three years, Micky and Blake had managed to stay together in foster care—ever since their mom had died of a drug overdose, leaving Micky and Blake with no one in the world except each other. Their mom had had big problems, but she had been their mom, and Micky still missed her. Blake didn't remember their mom all that well, though. He'd been less than two years old when she died.

For him, Micky was the only family he'd ever known. She'd protected him and kept him safe through eleven different foster homes, even the last one, where they had hit her and tried to hit Blake, and where they had sometimes refused to give them anything to eat. Stephanie had taken them away from the family as soon as she had found out—but now Micky wished she'd never told Stephanie what was happening.

"How are you doing back there, Micky?" Stephanie asked.

Micky shrugged. "Fine," she muttered. She'd done all the begging and pleading yesterday, when Stephanie had told her what was going to happen. She'd learned in her life there wasn't much point in arguing when people had made up their minds.

"You're just a stupid foster kid," a big kid on the school bus had told her once. Stephanie was Micky and Blake's caseworker, and she'd always been nice, but you never knew what people really thought. Maybe Stephanie thought she was just a stupid foster kid too.

"Here we are," Stephanie said, as she pulled into a driveway.

Micky looked out the car window and saw a two-story white house with a stone walkway and a flower garden. A girl was kneeling beside the flowerbed, pulling out weeds. She stood up and waved when she saw the car. She looked like she was about ten or eleven, a year or two older than Micky.

Stephanie got out of the car, and Micky opened the door and slowly got out as well. The summer air felt hot after the car's air conditioning, and she squinted at the bright sunshine, wishing she could climb back into the cool car and hide.

The girl ran over to the car. "I'm Lisa," she said. "You must be Michelle."

"Micky," said Micky. "Nobody calls me Michelle."

"Mrs. Hill is going to call you Michelle," Lisa said. "Sorry. She just doesn't like nicknames."

"What's she like?" Micky asked.

"Nice," Lisa said, "but strict sometimes. Tons better than a lot of places I've been, though."

Stephanie had gotten Micky's suitcase out of the trunk. "Let's go introduce you to Mrs. Hill," she said.

The three of them walked up the steps to the front door, and Lisa went in first.

The house was pretty nice. Micky could see that right away. She could see a kitchen toward the back of the house, and an older woman was coming toward her down the hall. The woman was tall, and her white hair was wrapped into a bun on the back of her head.

"Hello, Michelle," the woman said. "I'm Mrs. Hill. I'm glad to meet you."

Micky glanced at Lisa. She didn't try to correct Mrs. Hill about her name.

Over the next week, Micky got used to the routine at Mrs. Hill's house. Besides Lisa, two other girls, Shannon and Tori, also lived there. Mrs. Hill was a widow and had never had children, even though she had wanted them, so now she took in foster kids. Micky shared a bedroom with Lisa, while Shannon and Tori shared another room. Micky really liked Lisa, and Tori was funny, but she hadn't made up her mind yet what she thought about Shannon.

And Lisa was right about Mrs. Hill—she was nice, but she could be strict. She believed in good manners and insisted that all the girls help out with cooking and chores. Micky didn't mind that. She liked learning to cook, and she liked helping take care of the house. Mrs. Hill seemed to think Micky was worth something and not just a "stupid foster kid," and Micky liked that too.

In fact, Micky thought she could be happy at Mrs. Hill's house if it wasn't for Blake not being there. She missed Blake a lot, and she worried about him. She wanted to know where he was and if his new family was giving him enough to eat. She wanted to make sure nobody was hurting him or being mean to him. The longer she was away from him, the more nervous she got.

"Why couldn't you take my little brother, too?" she'd asked Mrs. Hill on the second night.

"I don't take boys, dear," Mrs. Hill had said. "I don't know anything about raising them and they're better off with someone who does."

"But Blake would be better off with me," Micky had said. "And he's only four years old. He's not like a big boy."

Mrs. Hill had just shaken her head, given Micky a hug, and told her to go brush her teeth.

Micky was having trouble sleeping and she hardly ate anything. She'd been so hungry when she first came to Mrs. Hill's house that she had eaten everything she'd been given, but now she had lost her appetite. She was too worried about Blake.

"What's your problem, anyway?" Shannon asked one evening after supper. The two of them were clearing the dishes off table in the dining room. "All you do is mope around. You think you're too good for the rest of us?"

Micky shrugged. "That's not it. I just miss my brother."

"Yeah, well, that's life," Shannon said. "Besides, you're probably better off without a snot-nosed brat following you around."

"Shut up, Shannon!" Micky said. "You don't know what you're talking about."

"I know enough." Shannon was chewing gum and she blew a big bubble in Micky's face.

Almost without thinking, Micky slapped her across the face. She was angry, she missed Blake, and she just wanted Shannon to go away.

Shannon glared at her. She dropped the cup she was holding and slapped Micky back.

The next thing Micky knew, the two of them were rolling around on the kitchen floor, hitting each other. Shannon had a handful of Micky's hair and was yanking at it. Tears sprang into Micky's eyes. She tried to get Shannon to let go by digging her fingernails into the back of Shannon's hand.

Neither of them heard Mrs. Hill come into the kitchen until she shouted at them, "Get up off that floor this instant!"

Shannon let go of Micky's hair and they rolled away from each other. Micky sat up, rubbing her head. She was crying.

"This is unacceptable behavior," Mrs. Hill said. "Both of you will get up, finish clearing the table, and then go straight to your rooms for the rest of the night. If I find either of you breaking the rules like this again, we will need to discuss more serious consequences."

"Like what?" Micky asked.

Mrs. Hill looked at her. "If this kind of behavior keeps up," she said, "we would need to discuss whether this is the right place for you."

Micky had heard that kind of thing before. Something always seemed to go wrong at foster homes. She would mess up, and then the foster parents would say they couldn't have her there anymore.

She finished clearing the table without saying anything and without looking at Shannon, then went up to her room and lay facedown on her bed. Maybe it would be a good thing if she were sent away. Maybe then she could be with Blake again.

The next day, when Mrs. Hill and the other girls were working in the garden, Micky slipped into the house and called Stephanie.

"I hear you've been having some trouble there," Stephanie said, but Micky didn't want to talk about the fight with Shannon, so she ignored the comment.

"I want to talk to Blake," she said. "You said you were going to get me a phone number so I could call him."

"Yes." Stephanie said and gave Micky the phone number. She tried to say something else, but Micky interrupted her.

"Thanks, Stephanie. This is great. Gotta go."

She hung up and looked down at the number she had written on her wrist. Her heart was pounding as she picked up the phone again and dialed the number. Was Blake happy? she wondered. Did he miss her?

She listened to the phone ring again and again, but no one answered, and the call finally clicked over to voice mail.

"You have reached Dale and Rita Coleman," a woman's voice said. "No one is available to take your call, but leave your name and number and we'll get back to you."

Micky hung up again. She knew the name and the phone number of Blake's foster family now, but she still hadn't talked to Blake.

By that evening, she had tried the number six times, but there was never any answer. Mrs. Hill had a computer, and she sometimes let the girls use it, so after supper, Micky got permission to use it for a few minutes. She told Mrs. Hill that she wanted to check her e-mail to see if any of her friends from school last year had written to her, but that wasn't true.

She sat down at the computer and typed the phone number into the search engine. The page of search results appeared. At the top of the page was the name Dale Coleman with an address.

Micky's heart was pounding again. She typed the address into a map program. Blake's foster home was in a suburb, about seven miles away from Mrs. Hill's house. Micky printed the directions, then folded up the printed page and tucked it in the top of her sock. Before Mrs. Hill could ask what she was doing, Micky closed the Internet windows she'd opened and told Tori she could have a turn on the computer.

The next morning, before anyone else was awake, Micky got up and crept out of the house. Following the directions she had printed out from the Internet, she walked toward Blake.

As she walked, the sun rose higher in the sky, and the day got hotter. Micky was sweaty and wished she had something to drink, but she kept walking. She thought about Blake as she walked. He was the only person in the world who loved her, and she had been the only person who loved him.

When she reached the right street, Micky figured out which house belonged to the Colemans.

It was small and made of red brick, and a huge shady tree took up most of the front yard. As she got closer, she saw a bench swing hanging from one of the tree's lower branches. A woman was sitting on the swing, facing away from Micky.

Suddenly Micky froze. A little boy was sitting beside the woman, cuddled into her side as she read him a book. Micky took a few steps closer, staring hard at the boy. His hair looked like Blake's, and he was the right size, and then the boy turned his face toward the woman, laughing, and Micky saw for sure that it was him.

She stopped walking. She'd been so worried that he wouldn't be able to survive without her, but he looked fine. He looked happy. She didn't know what to do next. Should she turn around and walk back to Mrs. Hill's house and let Blake have his happy life with the Colemans?

Micky wrapped her arms around her stomach and hugged herself. Even though it was as hot as

ever, she felt suddenly cold. There was no one in the world who loved her now.

Maybe she'd made a noise, because the woman turned around and looked right at Micky.

"Yes?" the woman asked. "Do you need something?"

Blake turned around too, then, and when he saw Micky, he smiled. He threw himself off the swing and flung himself in her arms.

"Micky!" he yelled. "I missed you."

"I missed you too." She hugged him tight, feeling suddenly better than she had in days.

"Are you going to stay with me here?" Blake asked.

Micky turned to look at the woman.

"Blake, come here," the woman said. "We need to go in the house and make a phone call."

"I want to stay with Micky," Blake said, but Mrs. Coleman shook her head.

"Go in the house, Blake. I'll be there in a minute. Micky will stay out here and wait for us."

Reluctantly, Blake let go of Micky and walked toward the house. Mrs. Coleman waited until he was gone and then turned back to Micky.

"How dare you come here?" she asked. "Blake was happy. He would have forgotten about you. We love him. How could you be so selfish?"

Micky felt like Mrs. Coleman had hit her. "But I love him too," she said. "And he's my little brother."

Mrs. Coleman wasn't listening. "Just stay here," she said. "I'm going to call Stephanie to come get you."

Mrs. Coleman turned and strode into the house, letting the door bang shut behind her.

Micky collapsed on the bench swing and started to cry. She was exhausted from walking, and her emotions were all mixed up. She had been so happy to see Blake, but she didn't know to feel about what Mrs. Coleman had said. Was she selfish to want to see Blake? Would it really be better for him to never see her again?

She sat on the swing for a long time. Once, she looked up and saw Blake at a window, looking at her, but then Mrs. Coleman pulled him away. Eventually, Stephanie pulled into the driveway. She got out of her car and sat down on the swing next to Micky.

"Oh Micky." She put her arm around Micky and didn't say anything else for a while.

"I messed everything up, didn't I?" asked Micky. "I just wanted to see Blake."

"I know," Stephanie said. "I hated separating you. I couldn't find a family who was able to take you both. But then, two days ago, I got the name of a new family who want to take both you and Blake. In fact, they may even be interested in adopting you. I didn't say anything about it last night when I talked to you, because I hadn't confirmed it yet. I didn't want to get your hopes up for nothing. But I'd just gotten off the phone with Mr. McGowan this morning when Mrs. Coleman called about you being here."

Micky started to cry again. The new family had been going to take her and Blake, and then she'd run away from Mrs. Hill's. Now they wouldn't want her anymore. "I really did ruin everything," she said.

"No," Stephanie said. "It's going to be okay. The McGowans still want to take you. I think you and Blake will be happy there."

Micky was afraid to hope. "Really?" she asked.

Stephanie smiled at her. "Let's go tell Blake," she said.

Micky jumped off from the swing. She knew that getting to know the McGowans would take time. She had been through too much in her life to hope that she and Blake would ever have a happily-ever-after ending to their story.

But maybe everything was going to be all right after all.

Kids in Foster Care

Micky and Blake are two examples of kids in foster care. They live with parents who aren't their birth parents because they don't have parents who can take care of them.

The word "foster" means to help grow or encourage. If a kid's parents (or parent) cannot take care of them, they may go into the foster care **system**. Foster care places kids in homes with foster parents who will take care of them—who will encourage them to grow up safe and healthy.

Understand the Word

A **system** is a set of things that work together to deal with a specific task or problem.

Foster parents can give kids a safe place to live when their home isn't safe. Foster parents can help kids with homework and make sure they eat well. Foster care isn't always perfect, and sometimes foster parents have problems of their own. But foster care can help many kids when their birth parents aren't able to take care of them.

More than half a million kids are in foster care in the United States. Many of these foster kids have stories that are a little like Micky and Blake's. Others have very different stories.

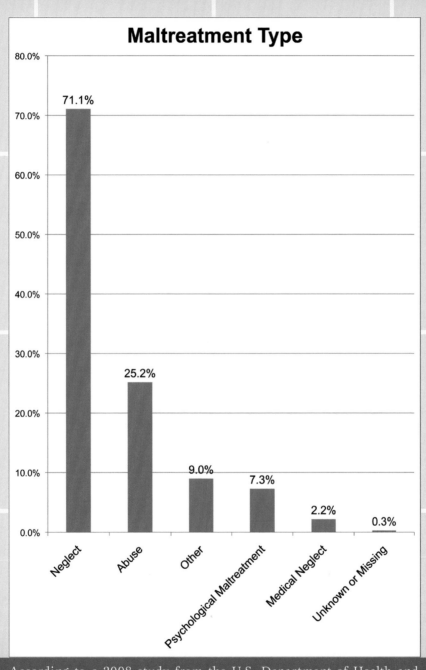

Maltreatment Type

According to a 2008 study from the U.S. Department of Health and Human Services, most cases reported to Child Protective Services were situations involving neglect.

Why Do Children Go into Foster Care?

Children go into foster care for different reasons. Sometimes their parents have died, as was the case with Micky and Blake, and they have no relatives who can step in and take care of them. Other times, children live in homes where their parents can't or won't give them the food they need—or they don't watch over their children and keep them from getting into dangerous situations. Some parents are unable to provide a safe place for their children to live. Other parents **abuse** their children. Parents who use drugs or drink too much alcohol may be more likely to do these things, which could mean their children will need to go into foster care. Sometimes, if a parent goes to jail, the children in the family may need to go into foster care.

Children need to be safe. If they aren't, Child Protective Services steps in. Sometimes, foster care is the answer for these children.

Understand the Word

Abuse means to hurt or treat someone badly.

What Is Child Protective Services?

Child Protective Services is a part of the government that looks into any **reports** of abuse and **neglect** of children. It also:

- provides help to children and families in their own homes.
- places children in foster care.
- helps older children in foster care cross the bridge into adulthood.
- places children in **adoptive** homes.

What Happens in Foster Care?

In foster care, people who aren't children's birth parents will take care of them in their own homes. Foster parents make sure children have enough food to eat and a safe home to live in. They can also help kids whose parents weren't taking care of them grow up in a place that is safe.

Understand the Word

Reports are when people say that something has happened.

Neglect is a lack of attention and care.

Adoptive has to do with parents who take a child into their family legally and raise him as their own.

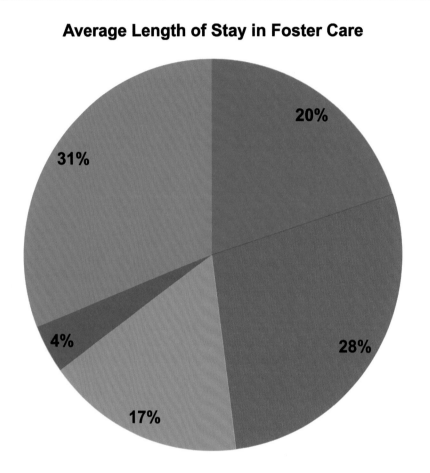

Average Length of Stay in Foster Care

20%

31%

28%

4%

17%

■ 1 to 2 years ■ 2 to 4 years ■ 5 years or more ■ Less than 1 month ■ 1 month to 1 year

Foster care does not last forever. As this chart shows, over half of children who enter the foster care system are in it for less than 2 years.

Most often, foster care isn't something that lasts forever. Many kids may go into foster care for a short time. Then they will return to their birth parents once their parents are able to care for their children. Some kids, however, are in the foster care system for their whole childhood, until they reach the age of eighteen. Others will live with foster parents only until they are **adopted**.

When a kid goes into foster care, he is assigned a caseworker, someone whose job it is to help that child. Stephanie is Micky and Blake's caseworker. Caseworkers like Stephanie place kids into different types of foster care. The goal of foster care is to give kids a place to live while their caseworker looks for a permanent home for them. Foster kids may return to their birth parents or move to a new home where they can stay permanently.

Here are a few examples of the different types of foster care:

- *regular foster care*: This is the most common kind of foster care. Kids in regular foster care live with foster parents until their caseworker can find them

> ### *Understand the Word*
>
> **Adopted** means to take a child legally into a family for the rest of her life. By law, that child will now be a part of that family, just as though she had been born into it.

a permanent home. Kids in regular foster care may move to a few different foster homes before they find the right place to stay. Moving around can be very hard on children, but sometimes it cannot be avoided.

• *short-term emergency care*: Emergency foster care gives kids a place to live when they need to leave their birth parents' home quickly. This can happen when a parent dies or when there is a problem at home that happens suddenly. Kids usually only need to stay in emergency care for a short time. Then they will either go back home or they will move to a longer-term home.

• *foster/adoptive care*: In some cases, foster parents care for a foster child they want to eventually adopt as their own.

Who Is in Foster Care?

Kids of every age and race are in foster care. Out of the half million children in foster car, a little more than 100,000 are between one and five years old. Another 100,000 or more of the kids in foster care are be-tween the ages of six and ten. Most of the kids in fos-

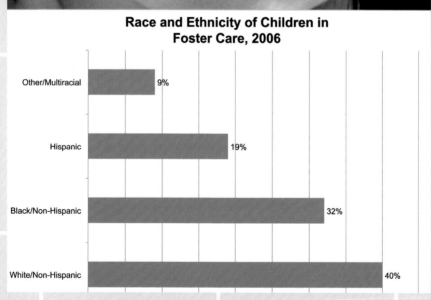

Race and Ethnicity of Children in Foster Care, 2006

Other/Multiracial	9%
Hispanic	19%
Black/Non-Hispanic	32%
White/Non-Hispanic	40%

Kids of all races end up in the foster care system. According to Childwelfare.gov, the trends from 2000 to 2006 showed a decrease in the numbers of White and African-American children entering foster care, while the percentage of Hispanic kids increased.

ter care are between the ages of eleven and fifteen, and about 80,000 are between sixteen and eighteen years old.

Kids with many different backgrounds are in foster care. There are more White kids in foster care than kids from any other **racial** background. African-American kids are the next largest group within the foster care system, but kids from every race are in foster care.

There are more boys than girls in foster care, as well, but not by much. 52 percent of all children in foster care are boys, and 48 percent are girls.

Foster care helps kids of all kinds. There is no "type" of kid who is in foster care. Kids of many different backgrounds all get help through the foster care system.

What Do Foster Parents Do for Foster Kids?

Foster parents give their foster children the things they need to grow up healthy and safe. They make sure

Understand the Word

Racial has to do with a group of people who all have the same background in terms of where they come from and what they look like.

There is no certain type of kid in foster care—both girls and boys of all ages and races end up in the foster care system.

Foster parents need to provide a safe, loving, and healthy environment while they have a foster child. The child will need healthy meals, doctor visits, and help with school work just like any other kid.

foster children are eating healthy foods. Their home must be a safe and **positive** place for a kid to live.

Foster parents will need to make sure that their foster child goes to the doctor and the dentist. If foster kids are having trouble with schoolwork, foster parents help them.

Many times foster kids have a lot of feelings that are hard to deal with alone. Foster parents need to be understanding of a foster child's emotions, and make sure to help them when it's possible. Foster parents also need to be good role models for foster kids, even if they are only in children's lives for a short time. Many times, foster care organizations help foster parents learn these things.

> ### Understand the Word
>
> Something that is **positive** makes a person feel good about himself. It helps him learn healthy habits and have good attitudes about life in general.

How Do People Become Foster Parents?

To become foster parents, adults let Child Protective Services know they are interested in becoming foster parents. They fill out applications. They go to meetings to get information about what it takes to be a foster parent. Child Protective Services will talk to them and ask them many questions, to make sure they can handle the needs of foster children. Someone from Child Protective Services will visit their home to make sure it is a safe place for children. They may be required to take classes before becoming foster parents.

Many different people become foster parents. No one type of person will make a better foster parent, just as no one type of person makes a good parent.

To become a foster parent, a person needs to:

- be old enough (some places this means at least 21 years old, other places it means at least 18).
- be in good health.
- have a job or be retired.
- have a house or home with enough space for foster kids.
- let people like caseworkers come into their home from time to time to see if everything is okay.
- have enough time to be a good foster parent and to work with caseworkers or other people from Child Protective Services.
- be able to work toward getting their foster child into a permanent home.

Children Exiting Foster Care, 2006

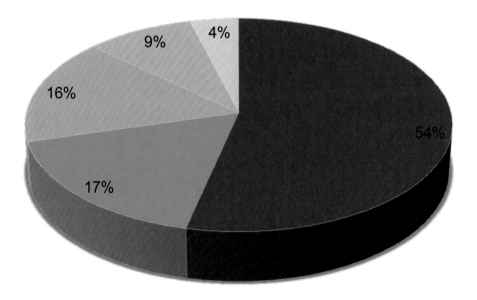

4%

9%

16%

54%

17%

■ Reunited with parents ■ Adopted ■ Went to live with relative ■ Emancipated ■ Other

Foster care does not last forever. Over half of the kids in foster care eventually go back home to their parent(s) or guardian.

If a person meets all of these requirements, they may be allowed to become a foster parent. Being a foster parent can be a lot of work, but it's also a great way to help a kid who is having a hard time.

How Do Kids Leave Foster Care?

Foster care isn't meant to last forever. Kids will leave the foster care system in different ways. The goal of foster care is always to find a place for a kid to live that will be their home permanently.

Here are a few ways that kids leave the foster care system:

- Birth parents will be able to take their child back if they can prove they can take care of children now. Most kids who are in foster care will go back to their birth parents home.
- If a child is adopted, parents who are not his birth parents take care of him as if he is their own. An adopted child becomes a permanent member of his new parents family.
- Some kids in the foster care system will end up living with a relative. A grandparent, for example,

might take their grandchild if the child's parents can't take care of her.

• A foster child may leave the system to live with someone who is not related to him. This person becomes their **guardian**.

• Some teens in foster care may be allowed to live on their own. These teens might have their own place to live and get help finding a job. Teens living on their own don't have a guardian or foster parents.

Understand the Word

A **guardian** is someone who is legally responsible for raising a child. He or she is not the same as an adopted parent, however.

Questions to Think About

1. What do you think would be the hardest thing about being in foster care?

2. Why do you think the older kid on the bus said something mean to Micky? Why are kids mean to other kids who are in different situations?

3. Do you think Micky was being selfish when she went to Blake's foster home? Why or why not?

4. How would you feel if you had to live with Mrs. Hill? Why?

5. Do you think Micky and Blake will be happy in their new home? Why or why not?

Further Reading

Atkins, Linda. *Jamaica and Me.* New York: Random House, 1998.

Fields, J. *Foster Families (The Changing Face of Modern Families).* Philadelphia, Penn.: Mason Crest Publishers, 2009.

Nelson, J. *Families Change.* Minneapolis, Minn.: Free Spirit Publishing, 2005.

Nelson, J. *Kids Need to Be Safe: A Book for Children in Foster Care.* Minneapolis, Minn.: Free Spirit Publishing, 2005.

Wilgocki, J., Wright, M. K., Geis, A. I. *Maybe Days: A Book for Children in Foster Care.* Washington, D. C.: American Psychological Association, 2002.

Find Out More on the Internet

Casey Family Programs
www.casey.org

Child Welfare League of America
www.cwla.org

Foster Care Statistics—ChildWelfare.gov
www.childwelfare.gov/pubs/factsheets/foster.cfm

Foster Club
www.fosterclub.com

Foster Parenting
www.fosterparenting.com

KidsHealth.org—Foster Families
kidshealth.org/kid/feeling/home_family/foster_families.html

National Foster Care Month
www.fostercaremonth.org

Orphan Foundation of America
www.orphan.org

The websites listed on this page were active at the time of publication. The publisher is not responsible for websites that have changed their address or discontinued operation since the date of publication. The publisher will review and update the websites upon each reprint.

Index

abuse 30–31
adopt 25, 31, 33–34, 42–43
African-American 35–36
alcohol 30

birth parents 28, 31, 33–34, 42

caseworker 10, 33, 40
Child Protective Services
29–31, 39–40

Department of Health and
Human Services 29
drugs 30

emotions 24, 39

foster care
    foster/adoptive 34

regular 33–34
short-term emergency 34
system 28, 32–33, 35–37, 42

guardian 41, 43

Hispanic 35

jail 30

neglect 29, 31

race 34–37
role models 39

school 10, 19, 38–39

Picture Credits

Fotolia.com:
    Anyka: pg. 38
    Galina Barskaya: pg. 37
    Kellie Folkerts: pg. 35

To the best knowledge of the publisher, all images not specifically credited are in the public domain. If any image has been inadvertently uncredited, please notify Harding House Publishing Service, 220 Front Street, Vestal, New York 13850, so that credit can be given in future printings.

About the Authors

Sheila Stewart has written several dozen books for young people, both fiction and nonfiction, although she especially enjoys writing fiction. She has a master's degree in English and now works as a writer and editor. She lives with her two children in a house overflowing with books, in the Southern Tier of New York State.

Camden Flath is a writer living and working in Binghamton, New York. He has a degree in English and has written several books for young people. He is interested in current political, social, and economic issues and applies those interests to his writing.

About the Consultant

Cindy Croft, M.A. Ed., is Director of the Center for Inclusive Child Care, a state-funded program with support from the McKnight Foundation, that creates, promotes, and supports pathways to successful inclusive care for all children. Its goal is inclusion and retention of children with disabilities and behavioral challenges in community child care settings. Cindy Croft is also on the faculty at Concordia University, where she teaches courses on young children with special needs and the emotional growth of young children. She is the author of several books, including *The Six Keys: Strategies for Promoting Children's Mental Health.*